DITCH THE BUILDING

7 Ways the Church Could Go Rogue and Fix Everything

NICK MAY

Σ ENERGION

ISBN: 978-1-63199-672-6

Energion Publications
P. O. Box 841
Gonzalez, FL

pubs@energion.com

This book is dedicated to the congregations that were displaced by Hurricane Michael. Now you are truly the church.

Table Of Contents

Architecture
Hierarchy
Organism
Quorum
Livelihood
Butterflies
Juggernaut

"Sir," the woman said, "I can see that you are a prophet. Our ancestors worshiped on this mountain, but you Jews claim that the place where we must worship is in Jerusalem." "Woman," Jesus replied, "believe me, a time is coming when you will worship the Father **neither on this mountain nor in Jerusalem**. You Samaritans worship what you do not know; we worship what we do know, for salvation is from the Jews. Yet a time is coming and has now come when the true worshipers will worship the Father in the Spirit and in truth, for they are the kind of worshipers the Father seeks. God is spirit, and his worshipers must worship **in the Spirit and in truth**."

—John 4:19-24

A NOTE FROM THE AUTHOR

I didn't write this to pick a fight. Despite my Irish tracksuit and the look on my face, I actually dislike conflict very much. In truth, I almost didn't write the book at all. I was afraid of what my former mentors and church friends might think if I did. So I wrote a different book first (also about church-world). That one was more subtle. Less informed. Passive-aggressive, even. Okay, so maybe I *am* picking a fight.

In the pages to follow, you may be tempted to judge me as unduly crass or garishly irreverent. I assure you I am, at best, only *one* of those things. My words—whether four-lettered or foul-tempered—are meant to illuminate the absurd little battles for which we raise our banners. Think of any verbal or visual offenses hereafter as clever traps set by yours truly.

I am (was) a world-class church-goer and defunct church planter. Those are my only credentials. I pen this treatise to those in the path of the pendulum. To them that stand at the crux of greatness and obscurity, having yet to choose the latter…

NM

ARCHITECTURE

I'll say it—the church was never meant to have buildings. Not ever. The very fact that we do is probably the single greatest missed point in human history (unless man nipples actually *do* something). It's borderline as bad as the Israelites needing that golden calf...

What if, instead, you had to invite someone into your home to share the Jesus story with them? Cold. No five-step onboarding system. No curriculum. No invite cards. No pastoral backup. Just you, whatever translation of the Bible you're least bothered by and the best excuse for hospitality you can manage to cobble together on the spot.

It's a scary proposition—being 100% responsible for someone's introduction to the gospel message (let alone their discipleship). Can you imagine someone imposing that sort of expectation on you? He would have to be the kind of person who could simultaneously elevate and abolish the need for holy ground by fulfilling its purpose in himself and creating living temples out of human beings. Ludicrous, right?

I was sitting in Starbucks one morning, probably plotting some safe way to further my influence by book-authoring or YouTubing, when an obviously foreign family caught my eye. I watched as they ordered drinks and sat down next to me. What followed was a scenario many Christians are familiar with. I felt a white-hot flash of conviction—the likely self-imposed notion that I was supposed to *do* something. Approach them. Strike up a very unsolicited conversation.

The next ten minutes was an internal battle waged between the part of me that believes in following sudden urges and the part that reasons with the former, convincing me I'm not actually feeling what I think I'm feeling. Whichever was true, I stayed put, glued to my spot at the watering hole.

I share this cautionary tale, not for its utility to illustrate guilt or regret, but for the greater lesson it taught me about how ill-equipped I was to do anything *but* sit there. Please understand, I blame no one but myself for where I was in that moment. Because the truth is, I was beginning to realize that my natural course of action would have been to extend an invite to a church I was presently attending but with which I was quickly falling out of infatuation…

It was then that it occurred to me. My entire gospel strategy was one based on a crutch. The crutch of having a clubhouse to do all the work for me, so long as I could get warm bodies in the door. And it was actually crippling me.

I feel it's important to note that many of my close friends and family came to know Christ through the vehicle of a church building (for which I am eternally grateful). Had there not been a physical space for them to go to, I'm not sure they would have stumbled upon the truth themselves and been discipled by mature Christians otherwise. My Calvinist friends would say that depends on the status of their election. I say it depends on how many believers were in their immediate circle of influence at the time and exactly how equipped those folks were to act independently from a church.

The problem of church architecture isn't new. It may look different, but it's not unique to today. In the West, church buildings have always been important to the function of a church body (note the difference between the two). They connected communities together in a way no other construct could, until perhaps the internet.

Neighborhoods and communities have always seen a need for physical spaces where people from similar walks of life can meet and fellowship. I get that. And until the turn of the century, it didn't take coercion on the part of the pastor or staff to get members to invite others inside. It was more of a common sense extension of courtesy. "Hey, we're friends—I noticed you're in need. I know a place with people like us. It's close by, and they have donuts."

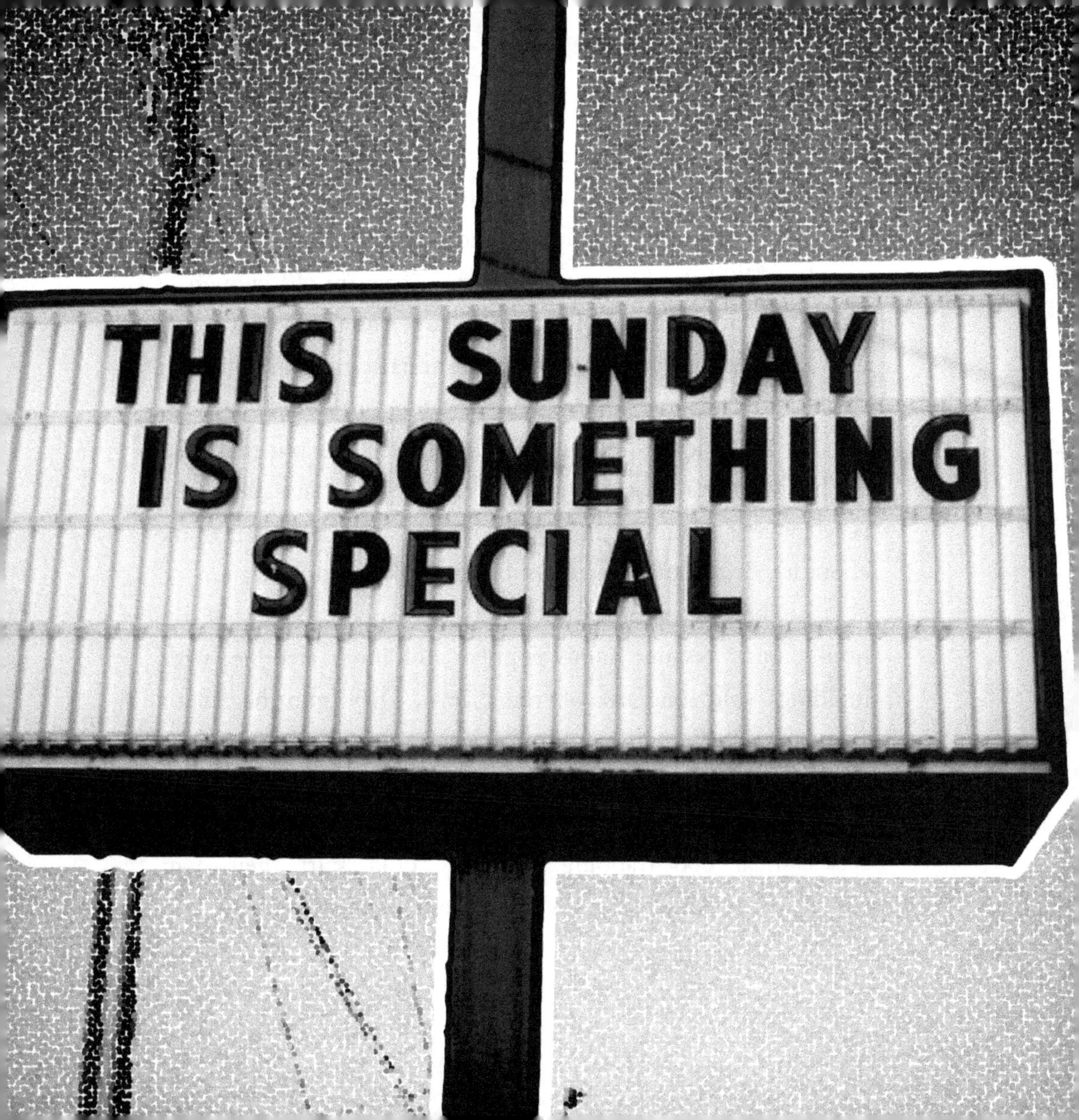
THIS SUNDAY
IS SOMETHING
SPECIAL

Even though the church of the late '90s could have existed outside the four-walled structure and done fine, there was still this demand for bricks and columns and pulpits and steeples. Think back a couple decades, if you're old enough... Do you remember a particularly large number of upstart churches outside the traditional denominations? Can you even recall a new *denominational* church being christened? Maybe, but for me, they've always been here. Like the bones of the earth. Or towels. No one buys towels, you just have them (the very concept of purchasing towels is almost crude, if you think about it). Bricks are a status symbol. Proof that you're legit.

Then, something new began to happen. Not only did non-denoms become more popular and more credible, with buildings and budgets of their own, they also began to approach church programing differently. Some saw the importance of adapting their techniques to reach the "unchurched" (whatever that means). It was the era of ecclesiastical bootstrapping. Anyone could start their own congregation. All you needed was a soul patch and a dream.

Buildings and property were replaced with school cafeterias and Facebook. Names began dropping their denominational designators in favor of more innocuous buzzwords like *Elevate*, *Radiate*, *Transformation*, *Generation*, *Renovation*, *Innovation*—or anything else that makes a church sound like a sexy new college apartment—and for a brief moment in the early aughts, the Western church nearly broke free of the formula. Until it didn't…

Like everything else on Planet Zuckerberg, church became a product of relentless competition. A numbers game. If you thought religious organizations were immune to the curse of personal comparison that you and I wrestle with daily on social media, you're not paying attention. I launched a church satellite in 2014 that nearly went tits-up its first month because another church in the area was killing the Facebook game, and I couldn't cope. Here's the honest truth—I think (I hope) most pastors intend to grow their churches with the wholesome desire to help more people, but it isn't always that noble.

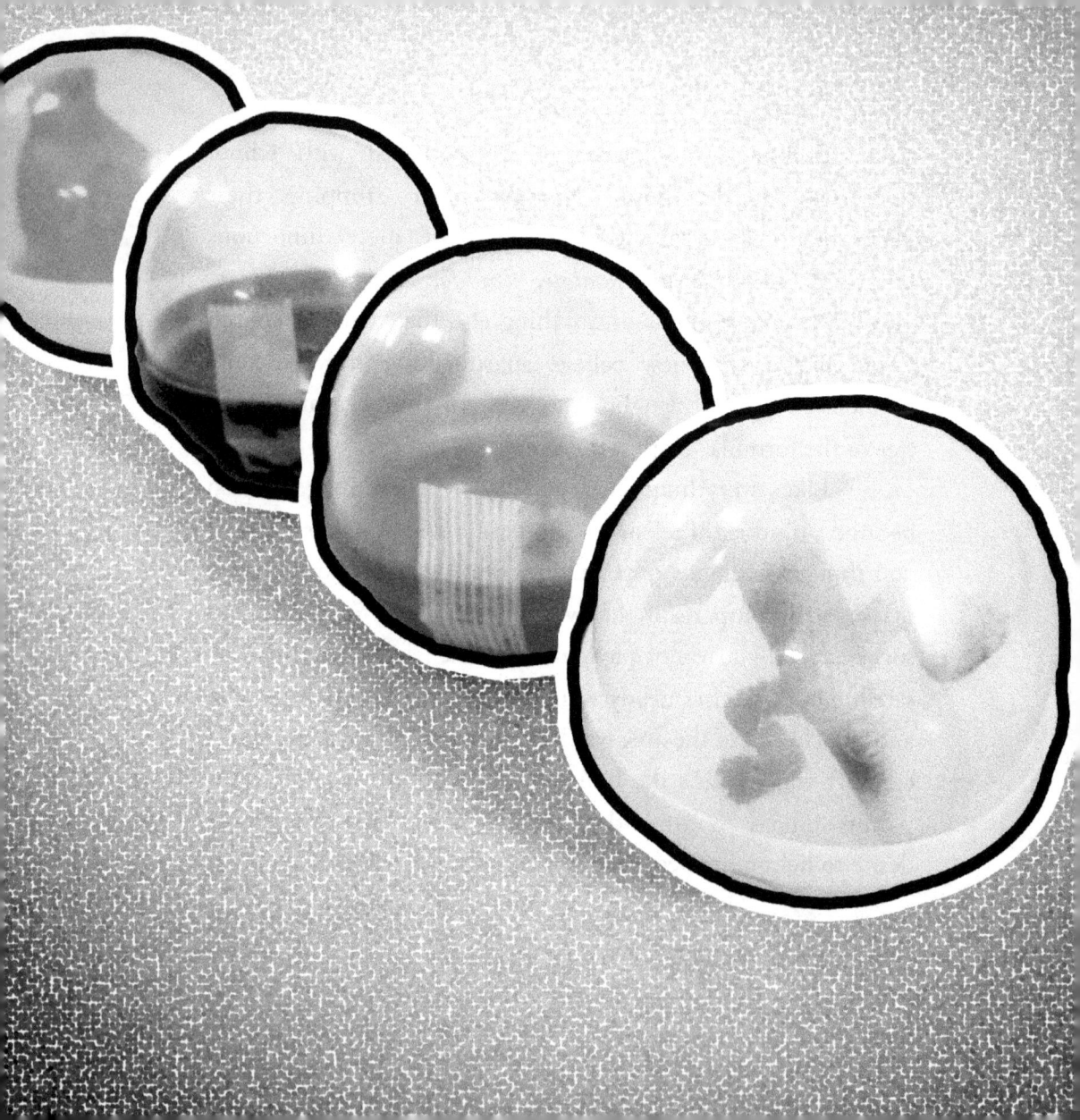

What you get instead is this veritable quarter machine, churning out one toy church formula after another. And who can blame them? When congregations all over the world are outgrowing their buildings and buying up new properties left and right just to make room, it's got to mean something right? I mean, right?! Why else would thousands of people flock to their local shoebox church every weekend to watch a GQ model (who they've presumably never met) tell them something they could have discerned for themselves, if they'd just read a Proverb every once in a while? Anyway, twenty-first century Christians have a problem (particularly those of us in the West). We've made a crutch of the clubhouse, rendering us corporately credible but independently impotent.

Disagree? Check your automated giving report. You're paying your tithe like an electric bill, but you've convinced yourself that giving twenty bucks to R.J. and his dog on the corner is bad stewardship. Check your calendar. You're showing up to every small group, volunteer night and leadership summit your church has to offer, but your own home is closed to the public. Check your kids—little Brayleigh and Jackson are making mountains of macaroni art in *KiDS Ministry*, but you're scared to tell your high-schooler to leave his bedroom door open when his girlfriend is over.

The point is, we've still got the training wheels on. Sure, we're staying upright, but we've never left the cul-de-sac, because the tires are flat, our knees keep hitting the handlebars, and we're peddling slower than we can walk. So what do all these flimsy analogies actually represent? First we need to take a step back and scope what physical church spaces used to look like versus what they look like now.

In the Old Testament temple, there was an outer foyer for preparing to enter, a large interior room for congregating and worship, and a super sacred inner sanctum, reserved for the most important intermediaries between you and God. I'll say again. An outer foyer, a large interior room, and a super sacred inner sanctum. Foyer, large room, inner sanctum … Anyone still need me to explain modern church architecture?

SANCTUM

L.G. ROOM

L.G. ROOM

FOYER

Now it's getting thick. So what happened to the O.T. temple? Bingo. In spite of Matthew 27:51 ("At that moment the curtain of the temple was torn in two from top to bottom,") Acts 17:24 ("The God who made the world and everything in it is the Lord of heaven and earth and does not live in temples built by human hands,") and pretty much all of John 14 ("That helper is the Spirit of Truth … You know him, because he lives with you and will be in you,") we never left. Our core doctrine still maintains that we meet God in a physical space, in which we prepare for a once-a-week encounter with the creator, via the channels of a high priest and a tribe of Levite musicians.

Quick detour. No one is advocating for disbanding the body of Christ (the Church with a capital C). If the title of the book didn't clue you in, I'm not sure the rest will do much more for you, but the point isn't giving up gathering together. The point is to finally shirk off the ways in which we've institutionalized the church. In particular, I'm talking about our modern day temples here. The very architectural model of Old

Testament God-encounters. And hey, if it only takes us two thousand years to course correct, better late than never.

What if you woke up tomorrow, and there were no more church buildings in your city? Like a game designer deleted them all from the map. I'm including mobile church favorites like schools, wedding venues, movie theaters and big empty storefronts that have to be vacated six weeks a year for *Halloween City*. Where would all the Christians go? What if the whole game changed overnight? How would people assemble to form the Voltron of counted heads, tithe checks and social media posts that churches need for validation?

Logistically, it really wouldn't be that odd (or at least it shouldn't be). And if you're anything like me and would love to see the church become more than a set of addresses, you should know, it's definitely within the realm of biblical possibility. But it's going to take an insane amount of trust on the part of pastors and leaders, who have a unique opportunity to tip the scales and help recapture what it truly means to be the church (not just be *a* church, or be *at* church).

Pastors and leaders—a lot of action in the steps that follow will rely heavily on you. The people you currently lead will need to understand why you're doing what you're about to do, and why they should be a part of it. That's on you. I can't do it for you. Somehow, you've won enough of their trust to call yourself their leader. Now you're going to have to help them understand their inherent identity as ministers, themselves. An identity the institution has stunted for a generation. A century. A millennia. You might even have to take the blame...

Modern pastors love practical. And this book isn't just about turning phrases or criticizing a system. It's about action. If you're not here to change something, or the words in these pages have already caused you too much grief, you should probably stop. Give the book to someone with nothing to lose. This challenge is for barefoot, black-eyed misfits who don't care about a nameplate on their office door. So, if you're still here, this is number one...

1. Ditch The Building

You don't need it. The most effective church is the one that exists within the crevices. Sell that brick box you're so dependent on (and not to another church). Don't say "It's not that easy..." Just do it. Tell the elders they've done a tremendous job helping you grow the church right out of its need for a building, and that their jobs are changing from advisors to servant-leaders. Put a sign out front, put some pictures on Craigslist, and turn off the lights.

Oh, and one last thing. In order to take this step and those to follow, you're going to have to do some things. You're going to have to give away your influence, your power, your platform. You're going to have to become invisible and follow Jesus to the back of the line. You might even have to wield a plunger once in a while. And there's only one way to accomplish it all—you're going to have to fire yourself.

HIERARCHY

> "Preach the gospel, die, and be forgotten."
> —Nikolaus Zinzendorf

There was a time when a pastor was the most vanilla-looking dude in the room. They wore suits from Men's Wearhouse, lived on the grounds and had wives that looked like Barbara Bush. They seemed older. Less concerned with appearances. I don't mean to say that made them better by any means, but it certainly made them more approachable. When

17

the pastor is the most fashionable person on Sunday (besides his spouse), it sort of narrows the range of common ground. Especially when they feel the need to reaffirm from the stage each week exactly *how* hot their wife is...

Anthony Bourdain once suggested that when the rock and roll subculture disappeared it morphed into the foodie movement, ushering in the era of the celebrity chef. I'll make the claim that the celebrity pastor slew the spiritual giant. He had to. There was simply no more room at the top. And that's literally a *giant* problem. If a pastor isn't interested in actively replacing himself, it's most likely because he feels minimized by the concept of lateral leadership (or fellow spiritual giants). But fame is a chef thing, not a pastor thing.

So what exactly is a spiritual giant? Ideally, it's a nobody to the world, but a HUGE somebody to a handful of people. Someone who disciples others. Someone who says, "Follow me as I follow Christ..." There used to be a lot more of them. They used to do what pastors were self-aware enough to know they couldn't do alone. Sunday school teachers, Bible study leaders,

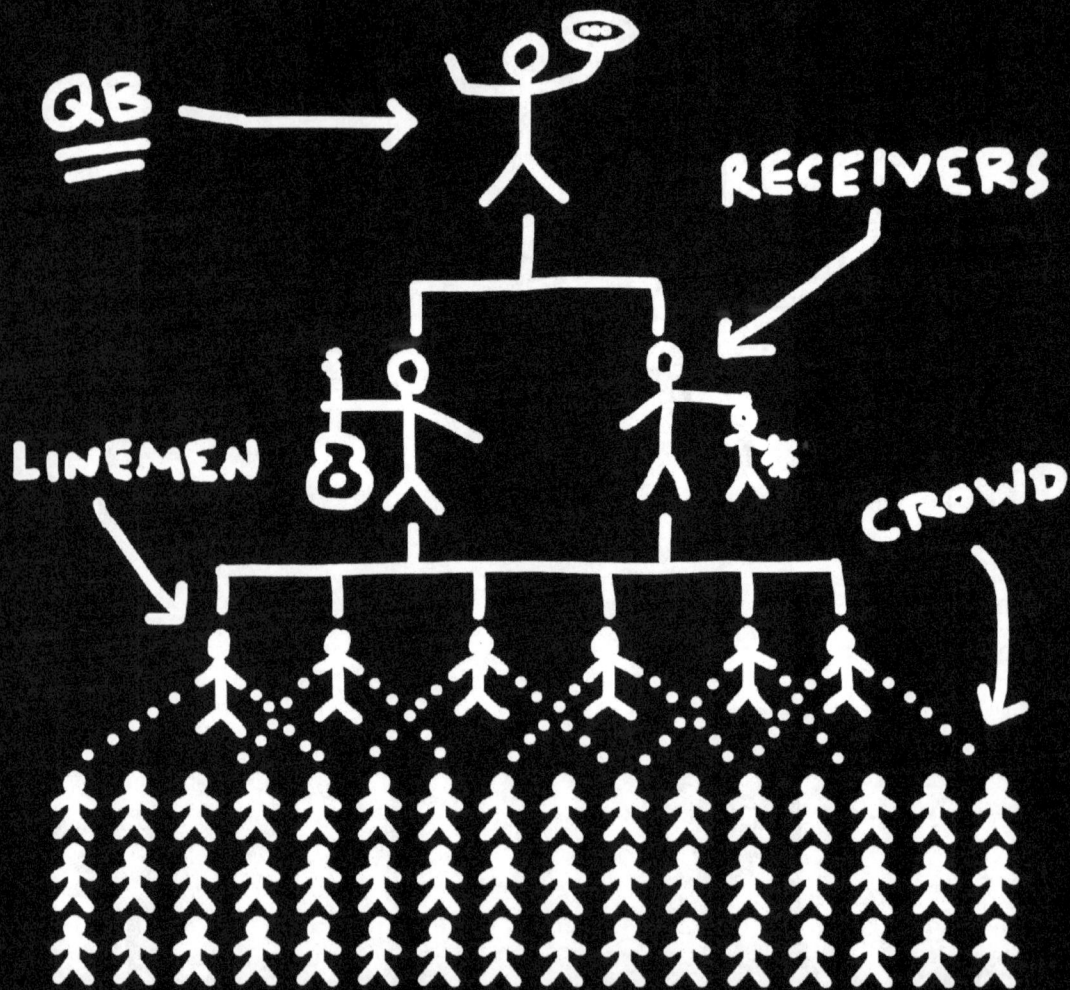

youth ministry volunteers, camp counselors, parents, nursery workers, elderly people, anyone who felt compelled and empowered to share their hope. They took others under their wing, taught them how to conduct themselves with spiritual accountability, and used that co-dependence to spur on their own relationship with God, because they had no choice.

If you look closely, you can still see their footprints—the spiritual giants. You might even stumble across one of their caves or hear them sleeping in the hills. If you poke one, it might stir a bit, or fully awaken. Some are well-fed and just need exercise. Some are starved or sickly. Others traded in their legs for stilts long ago so they could appear tall when called upon, and shrink away on command. A requisite for avoiding hibernation (wow, this is getting depressing).

So where have all the spiritual giants gone? Why does church hierarchy start with one guy at the top and trickle down, from greatest to least, until reaching the bottom where the congregation sits idle? It would be easy to say we just missed the boat (again), the way we did with architecture, that we somehow failed to see Jesus as the fulfillment of the priest rank or missed the concept of Christ living in us, cutting out the middle man between us and God. We could say that, but it would almost be too easy. Not enough obfuscation or mud between the bricks. So let's build a case that sticks.

Would it be inappropriate to suggest that maybe God had some pretty brilliant sub-plots in mind when he sent his son to die for all mankind? How weird would it be if there was a leadership lesson built into his sacrifice? What if part of Christ's purpose, after saying, "Ditch the priests, you have me now..." was to prepare his disciples to replace him on earth? Consider the design of his time here—he came, he taught, he left. Jesus had twelve guys ready to build the church within three years. After that, it was off with the training wheels. Why, then, are lead pastors death-gripping their positions instead of leading themselves into obscurity?

Here's the problem with the *one man* model of nearly every modern church—we're still shipping the idea of the Old Testament intermediary. The priest. The guy at the top with all the answers. The keeper of scriptures. The figurehead with the approved doctrine who we all look to. Listen, we need leaders. Leaders are imperative. Leaders teach us and correct us and disciple us. Leaders. *Leaders* do. Get it? Pastoring isn't a solo sport. Where did we get the idea that the church is a republic? Certainly not from any of Paul's letters.

If anything, the early church was a collective of like-minded people with a common directive. The purpose of a New Testament assembly, was to "spur one another on toward love and good deeds..." (Hebrews 1-:24). These were individuals who each knew the commission they had been given and were just as capable of acting independently as they were a unit. And yes, Paul wrote them a lot of instructions. He was definitely a dynamic leader, instrumental in spearheading and encouraging the movement, but he was still just an apostle. People listened because Paul spoke with authority and grace and humility, and his words were grounded in Christ, not in himself. He wasn't giving TED Talks. He was a Jesus parrot. A spiritual giant.

The church needs spiritual giants again. It needs to see its "one man" dethroned so true discipleship can finally take place. And the celebrity pastor should be the first to go. At least the construct of him. But what defines a "celebrity pastor" can actually be pretty tricky to discern, and often requires having an attuned eye for—No, I'm lying. Obviously. It's stupid easy to spot a celebrity pastor and only requires you to open your eyes long enough to flick through Instagram. They're the guys you see every day, systematically releasing little morsels of pseudo wisdom in overly dramatic ways. Usually with some sensual rust in their voice. Today the concept has far outgrown what we used to just see on TV or bookshelves.

What defines a celebrity pastor today has mostly to do with the context of *you*. They live in bigger houses than you, drive nicer cars than you and command the attention of hundreds or thousands every weekend from five-star platforms. If you listen closely, they're saying the same thing as Tony Robbins and Gary Vaynerchuck, only they're afraid to punctuate with expletives.

Celebrity pastors do not look like you. They look like celebrities, they talk like celebrities, they live like celebrities, they schmooze with other celebrities, and they build platforms for themselves so they can be visible ... like celebrities. And oftentimes the best argument in defense of these figures is that they have the eyes and ears of the world.

Is that why pastors only seem to know how to build megachurches? By appearances, it certainly seems like the goal of most modern congregations is to just get as insanely big as possible. In a nutshell, the strategy is to award one man with an audience of thousands, because we're banking on his monologues being good enough to do our job for us. Show me a pastor whose endgame isn't church brand growth, and I'll show you a man with a dying parish. Because people believe that evangelism is best served with a side of finesse and chiseled features, rather than individual commissions and gifts.

Practically speaking, this next play isn't nearly as sexy as ditching the building. Mostly because it hits wallets. It hits hubris. But it's the most like Jesus any of us could possibly look.

Firing yourself means you cease to have a platform. It means your life is devoted to promoting the pedestals of others. It means showing people how to follow you as you follow Christ, straight off the pages of history. To the bitter wastelands of unpopularity. This is what rogues do. This is how leaders give away their influence and empower people to disciple the world. All it takes is one step in the right direction—down.

MORE →

2. DITCH THE PLATFORM

You want exponential growth? Stop laboring under the delusion of top-down leadership. There doesn't need to be "a guy" and it certainly doesn't need to be you. A friend, a mentor—a spiritual giant—once told me that God ran the universe for a million billion years without me. Get out of the way so people can stop waiting for you to tell them what to do. Get three guys, go to Waffle House and eat together (the booths only fit four anyway). Hopefully your life paints a good enough picture of how to follow Christ. "Your cleansed and grateful life, not your words, will bear witness to what I have done."

—Matthew 8:4 (MSG)

So if we're on the same page, and we agree something has to structurally break at the top, then it begs asking, what is the purpose of church leadership centralized around one man? What is the point of a "lead pastor," and why are we so fixated on them being dynamic teachers who speak from platforms and lead from positions of privileged wisdom?

I've heard some objectively great leaders deliver some pretty atrocious messages (likewise, I've seen some amazing teachers lead their organizations into the ground). Why can't they, instead, be like AA batteries; working alongside other AA batteries to help empower the unit from some unseen compartment at the bottom? I'll wager a guess, but you're probably not going to like it. Maybe it's because the structure of Western church hierarchy—of celebrity pastors and dynamic leaders—makes for a pretty good franchise model. Organizations need CEOs, don't they? And what is the Western church if not a business?

ORGANISM

    I am the product of some pretty efficient church systems. I spent nearly ten years spiraling myself through concentric circles. Sort of the reverse of a juvenile delinquent. At the tender age of eighteen, I fell in love with a really wonderful church community (one I probably still have latent feelings for, if I'm completely honest). I started as a casual attender, then became a member, volunteer, lead volunteer, intern, part-time employee, full-time employee, project leader, department leader, until I found myself loading my entire life into a twenty foot trailer and moving back to my hometown, where my wife and I were to plant a satellite church campus. If that's not effective development, I don't know what is.

Now, was the problem that a great group of church leaders groomed me for ministry? Absolutely not. The problem was that I believed I had to be *the guy*. That's on me. What I was probably feeling at the time (and likely misinterpreting) was a heightened sense of purpose and empowerment to use my creativity to basically "Make straight the way of the Lord…" But "best practices" at the time weren't conducive to that sort of autonomy. Sure, the ultimate goal was to have every church member contributing within their gifts and passions, but modern formulas dictated that those contributions should be made within a prescribed template. "Love dogs? Great! Lead a dog-walking small group…" Get the idea?

The bottom line is that all churches eventually come face-to-face with the inevitable choice of whether they're going to be an organism or an organization. Many choose the former and become the latter. Some choose the latter and claim the former. And still others are functioning in their DNA as the

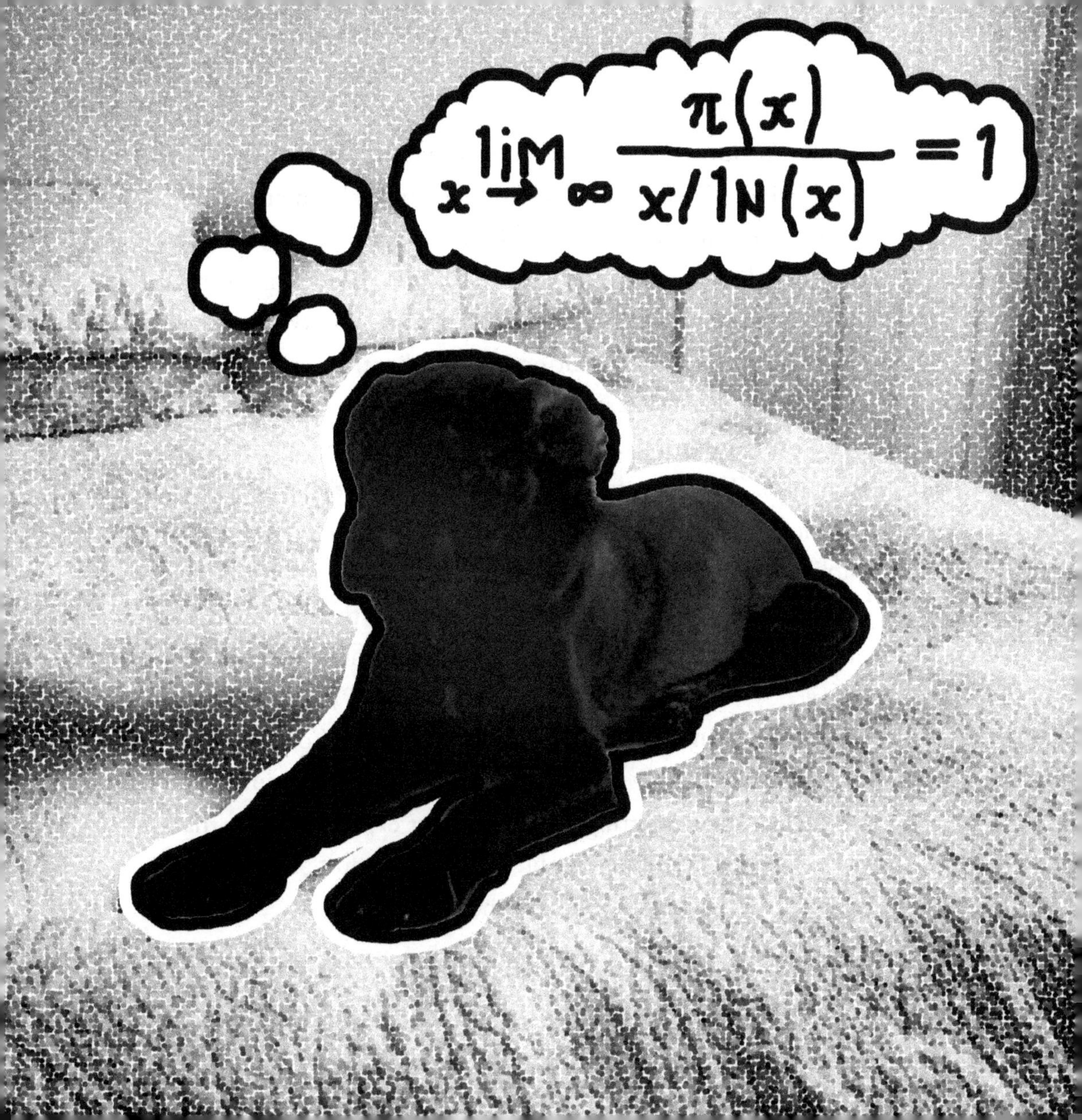

$\lim_{x \to \infty} \frac{\pi(x)}{x/\ln(x)} = 1$

former but for some deranged reason fight to be the latter. The point being, it's extremely rare for an assembly with any kind of self-imposed ambition to act like an organism, in the truest sense of the word. An organism has no payroll, no central office, no top-down hierarchical structure, no style guide or membership handbook. An organism is interdependent on its parts. It just does what it does.

Organizations, however, have lots of paper, ink, signatures. They like to write things down and create bylaws. They love a cookie cutter success formula. If it worked there, it's duplicatable here. I once asked Perry Noble if Newspring campuses had any sort of autonomy to make their own creative calls or adapt to their surrounding cultures when necessary. His answer… "We're like Chick-fil-A." Meaning, if you've seen one, you've seen them all. I understood it at the time (sort of). From a comfort and quality control standpoint. You don't want guests feeling like they're getting an inconsistent experience. But that's exactly what I'm talking about! Guests. Comfort. Experiences. All that business jargon, like it's a hotel chain.

The gospel isn't comfortable. Worship isn't predictable. The Holy Spirit isn't subject to quality control. Those three factors, alone, stand in opposition to this popular practice. It's the misconception that churches are competitors on some cosmic gameshow to earn your attention, so they can sell you on the single greatest *free* gift ever given. Churches actually believe they're competing with Disney World, Major League Baseball. Big screen blockbusters. The Super Bowl. I know, because I've said it and believed it, myself. But here's the ball-busting truth—Disney World will always be better. Always.

Competition and comparison with mainstream attractions will always be a losing battle in church world, because it's not our turf. It's not even our rulebook. If hitting emotional chords is the goal, we're just admitting that that we're down to manipulate. Sure, we might get close to manufacturing an American Idol moment, but that dissipates too.

Church staffs all over the world are going to insane lengths just to get people in the door every weekend. Ice cream trucks. Seizure-inducing stage designs. iPad giveaways. Snow

machines. Freaking petting zoos (I don't know, probably). All of which add up to another blind toss that misses the mark, in spite of what the numbers might imply. The common denominator is that most all of them fail to utilize the gut-crushing power of a simple testimony.

Ask yourself, maybe even as a pastor, what is the endgame? Fifty thousand weekly attenders? A hundred thousand? A branch in every nation? Every language? Would that make you feel like you've finally accomplished Matthew 28:19? What about a church in space?!

If the goal is world domination, it's going to take a pretty brilliant business plan. And probably a private military (pastors with that much gravity need a lot of security). You're going to have to terraform your church culture to every known and unknown geographical location on earth. We're talking the colonization of an entire planet. The tsunami-proof Sentinelese islanders of Andaman are going to have to see your J. Crew-clothed likeness projected on a twenty foot screen in their foyer while they eat donut holes and sip black bean water.

I won't say this expansive brand of global church creep isn't possible, but it's going to cost blood. And you're going to have to burn some people out along the way. That's right, burnout isn't passively enacted. It's not something that just happens to a person. Someone, somewhere, has to actively ignite the flint and tinder of promotion and neglect in order to set a good volunteer (or employee) ablaze.

If we're addressing the root problem caused by churches functioning as organizations, in most cases, it can always be traced back to promotion. Sure, there are plenty of other contributors, like how organizations tend to communicate impersonally or put you in a box, or always feel the need to make you a number, but it's promotion that kills. Hear me—church metrics can flourish even as people suffocate.

When *a* church puts ambition ahead of *the* church (the people), there's a problem. When kids ministry leaders are learning basic Bible stories for the first time, alongside the children they teach, that's probably an indicator of a discipleship deficiency. It's impatience, man, plain and simple.

It's "mile-wide, inch-deep" theology. The net of promotion is so vast that literally anyone who expresses interest or withholds protest can and most likely will be jettisoned to a position of leadership. And what happens to their further development? Some stick it out. Others later question whether they even believe in God. Did they do something wrong? I don't think so. They were just lost in a vast sea of aggressive expansion.

So let's tee up a possible solution here. What keeps an organism from becoming an organization. Better yet, what mutates an organism into an organization? The answer is in the word itself—organization. I can't prove the first church didn't use flowcharts or clever acronyms or an early version of Planning Center Online, but I can provide evidence that discipleship was priority number one. And the only way the church has any prayer of being that effective again, is if it stops tracking and measuring and starts making itself accountable to people until maturity is glaringly obvious in their lives, instead of on a spreadsheet. The next move makes absolutely no sense on paper. Because you won't be using any…

3. DITCH THE PAPER TRAIL

That's right. Cue heart palpitations. The genesis of every sellout scenario is when someone writes something down. The moment you try to document and measure effectiveness with numbers—the second you write down some prescribed bit of doctrine that you expect everyone to adhere to—is the exact moment you presume God must be napping and reach for the remote, outstretched in his open hand. And make no mistake, he'll let you take it. So stop counting. Stop graphing. Stop agonizing over syntax. Ditch the titles. Ditch the schedules. Ditch the checkboxes and memos and "connect cards" and be about people.

What have you honestly got to lose? So you won't be able to track whether you grew this year. Who cares! If people are spiritually healthy, the church grows. You just don't believe that. Or you don't want to be held personally accountable for keeping up with them yourself. Maybe you'd rather the system assimilate them on auto-pilot somehow, without dropping any through the cracks. But the church isn't an organization, it's an organism. And organisms just do what they do. If people are discipled, they will disciple others. If people are cared for, they will care for others. If people are valued inside an assembly, they will value the assembly. The church will lead, it will give, it will show up, and you won't need to understand how.

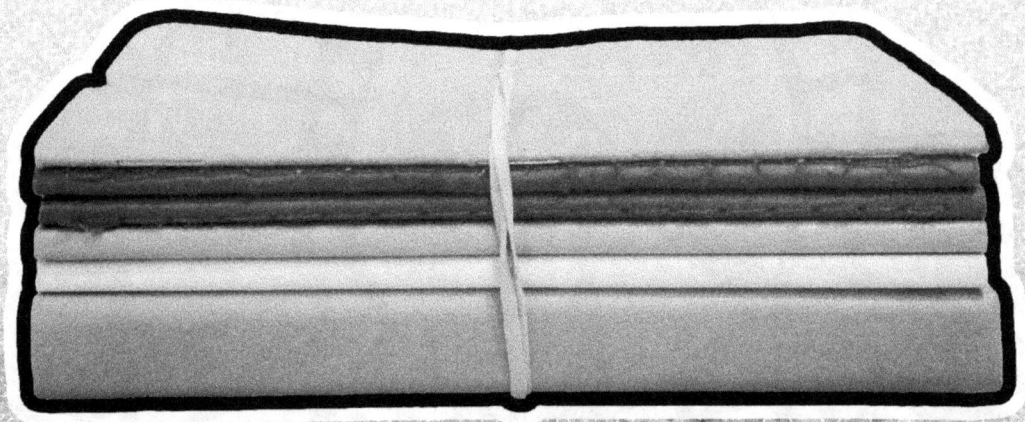

QUORUM

When I was a kid, I loved games like *Sim City*, *Rollercoaster Tycoon* and *Age of Empires*. It was the management aspect that really did it for me. Setting hundreds of individual characters to task and then overlording their productivity. There was something really satisfying about being in complete control of every moving piece. Knowing where everyone was, at any given time. Dominating my enemies. Bending tiny pixel people to my will. And the greatest part was that 95% of the activity could be monitored within a single frame. Sure, occasionally a stray unit would run off and get themselves killed, but they deserved it, you know?

It's this same kind of hyper-attentive head-counting that gets so many pastors and churches into deep water. If I can see you, great! I'll put you to work. If I can't see or control what you're doing, I'm either going to try to rein you in, or I'm going to decide you're expendable and cut you loose. You hear this kind of detachment talk in a staggering amount of churches these days. The whole idea that you are a finger in a cup of water, and as soon as you withdraw yourself, the gap closes in, like you were never there. Some pastors even practice a method of pretending everyone they meet is on their way out. Whether it's all for the sake of scaring people into sticking around or some sort of numb coping mechanism for preventing a pastor's feelings from being hurt, all it does is devalue people.

If the church only exists in metrics—time spent, money given, warm bodies in a room—then it only makes sense that all our efforts be spent doing everything in our power to corral as many people as possible into the same breathing space every

weekend. That way we can reinforce our values, collect dues and measure our resulting "effectiveness." But if a church, in theory, has no building, no central leader and no documentation, how can it ensure that all of its little lambs congregate and perform the way they're supposed to? How can it know the status of every single member during every single conceivable second of the day? How can it possibly remain spiritually and eternally accountable for everyone? Easy. It can't.

That's kind of the point, isn't it? Too much of the church's focus is on weekend attendance and how those weekly attendees respond on an 8.5 inch strip of paper. It's a favorite phrase of all church executives. One that drives the focus of their staff members and volunteers: "It's all about the weekend, baby." Sorry, but hard pass. That's not laser focus, that's tunnel vision. Perpetuate that kind of thinking among staff members, and volunteers and you can be sure it will eventually trickle into the general populace. Then the important thing becomes weekend spirituality, weekend stewardship and weekend sanctification. Basically your church produces A-students on Sunday and A-holes every other day of the week.

Again, the problem goes back to measuring things the way the world measures them. We can't just be the church. No, we have to be gathered in a building somewhere. We have to be worshipping corporately or listening to the preacher or showing our face every week at small group. And as a former pastor, I can say this with confidence, my greatest gauge for whether a given Sunday was good or bad, was always how many people were in the room. Sadly, no response to Jesus ever got me as jacked as a full house. Maybe I'm the only one who felt soaring victory or crushing loss based on numbers, but I doubt it.

I used to keep a little spreadsheet with all the names of every regular or semi-regular attender in my church. Each week I would either put an X by the names in attendance or leave the box blank. If someone collected three blank boxes, I would send them a text. I convinced myself I was just being a good shepherd. I was looking out for the spiritual development of my flock. Tending the garden. Whatever analogy works. But deep

down, all I wanted was a steady column of X's. All of these methods probably start with wholesome intentions, but Satan twists them, because they're an easy target for perversion. Dependence on numbers is a world thing.

I know pastors say, "Numbers matter, because numbers are people, and people are souls." Cool, let's focus on producing some stalwart souls and letting them duplicate organically. When Jesus fed the five thousand, and then again when he fed the four thousand, it was a ballpark estimate, at best. It just didn't matter. The important thing was that everyone was fed! Jesus never let numbers dictate the success of his ministry (most of which seems to have taken place outside).

So why do we do church meetings the way we do them? Why do we gather on Sundays? Why do churches funnel all their creative and monetary resources into the weekend. And why does the world respond so agreeably? Because we love a great system! Sunday is the day the world worships, and churches want to get in line with what's already socially accepted. We want to make it easy for people to follow Christ.

We want it to be fun and friction-free. But for who, just new believers? Yeah, we've streamlined that process into the dirt. It's so easy to meet Christ on a Sunday you'll practically forget you did! And you'll walk away none-the-wiser.

Apart from spoon-doping weekly church-goers with regular hits of calendar-based spiritual dependency, who else does the weekend system actively deprive? Well, practically speaking, everyone else who made it possible. Everyone who spent the prior six days doing their best to forget that the yoke is supposed to be easy and the burden light. Those who spent Saturday night rerouting in-ear monitors or cleaning haze machines or stapling LEDs to abstract foam core formations on the backdrop of the stage. Anyone who spent 60 hours trying to coax the maximum emotional impact out of a 5-minute video illustration. Anyone who got up early so their pastor wouldn't have to (yeah, I know, sorry...)

Simply put—if the church wasn't so focused on getting the weekend right, we'd do a much better job of being who we're supposed to be every other day of the week. We'd forget that Sundays are for "church business," and we'd invest that enthusiasm on a more even keel. We'd start to notice that any meeting we have is a chance to *be* the church. We'd realize that fellowship is what we need—not programming. Not bite-sized interactions in a controlled environment. Our accountability would shift. Instead of putting on our Sunday best (which often means much more than just clothing), we'd see every moment of the day as potentially observable by someone.

The church would exist in homes again. Around dinner tables. Over cups of coffee. Pints of beer. Every conversation you have would be a chance to sharpen somebody. The assembly wouldn't suffer, it would thrive. Because you, the former *church-goer-turned-church-lifer*, long for relationships, not obligatory meetings or more items added to your calendar. You don't need to be counted. And you, yourself, don't need to do any counting. Trust me, I get it. It can be exhilarating to be surrounded by a sea of people with their hands lifted. Even in spite of how we've twisted it, God can still work on Sundays. But exhilaration is not your calling. People are!

What if—and this is going to sound crazy—instead of trying to see how many human beings we can physically cram into one space at one time, for the sheer sake of validating our church gatherings—we actually tried to see how lean we could become and still be effective? "For where two or three gather in my name, there am I with them…" (Matt. 18:20). That's called a Quorum—*the minimum number of members of an assembly or society that must be present at any of its meetings to make the proceedings of that meeting valid.* There. *Lawyered.*

Here are two statements we can stand on, neither of which have anything to do with numbers: "By this everyone will know that you are my disciples, if you love one another…" (John 13:35) and "You will be my witnesses in Jerusalem, and in all Judea and Samaria, and to the ends of the earth…" (Acts 1:8). Statements we can't stand on: "It's all about the weekend…" "Get butts in seats…" "Measure everything…" Ready or not, here's challenge/opportunity number 4. A chance for you to really exercise your trust in God's ability and willingness to hold the universe together without you.

4. DITCH THE WEEKEND

By this point, your building is gone, your leaders are servants, you've gone paperless—why not shed your dependency on Sundays, too? Make it part of your collective culture to intentionally exist anywhere at any time. Teach and live discipleship until people forget the meaning of "going to church." You don't need to have all the kids under one roof anymore. Even Jesus blew up his own clubhouse. It was never in his design to keep everyone together. We'll go full Voltron in heaven. Until then, Sunday is cancelled. It's all about the week.

Of course, this kind of dangerous notion presents an interesting challenge. How do you bankroll a church that isn't held accountable to weekly offerings? How do you compensate those servant leaders for their time and wisdom? How do you appropriate funds on behalf of people who can't possibly discern generosity and good stewardship for themselves?

LIVELIHOOD

It's easy to talk about this stuff from the other side. It's easy for me to imagine you, the reader, as the hero of this story. In my head, you look just like Denzel, walking away from an explosion. What's not easy—and I understand why—is for you to ignore the fact that this might be your paying gig. Your livelihood. Whether you're the pastor or the receptionist, taking any one of these steps has the potential to leave you without a job. And I could romanticize about the church of Acts, pooling their resources to meet the needs of all the people, but we're

nowhere near that level of maturity yet (or again). We've become too accustomed to looking out for number one. What I will tell you is that if your church payroll is based on the generosity of people rather than the efficiency of systems, you won't miss a meal anyway.

I'll make this next part quick, because it sucks. Here's how church finances work. Unless you're part of some major convention—Baptist, Methodist, Catholic, etc—you're probably only supported from within. That means things like bills, payroll and programming are all funded by the weekly or monthly donations of your people. A lot rides on maximizing those opportunities for members to invest. I was once a part of a church that experimented with just placing the offering buckets at the exit doors one Sunday. A few people almost didn't get paid that week. It's that big of a deal on Sundays. And there better be multiple ways in which to give, including online or via text message. It's also important that people are aware of any fancy automated giving options (you know, in case they go on vacation and forget to pay their tithe bill).

That's what it was for me—a bill. And I was good at paying it. I was so efficient, in fact, I could do it without even thinking. And my bank account barely felt it. That was a huge problem. It was so easy for me to tithe, it stopped meaning anything. My motivation to give exactly ten percent of my monthly income was based solely on two things: I was convinced it was Biblically mandated for me, and I needed a way to help people without touching them. It was only when I realized tithing is a matter of the law[1] that I was able to see how strange my motivations truly were. As a follower of Jesus, I am not bound to the law—the rules established by God in the Old Testament for Jews to observe and follow to the letter.

Churches like to play it real cool with this theology, walking a careful line between demand and grace. It's one of those areas of scripture we keep defending as enduring moral law, when it's pretty blatantly ceremonial. We like it. It's useful —almost like we're telling Jesus, "Na, we're good. Let's keep up the standard of rules you came to complete." We are essentially

---

[1] Matthew 23:23

aspiring to be Old Testament Jews. And the most alarming part about this paradigm is that it's still the church's bread and butter. We still use the word "tithe" (tenth) as the principal unit of measurement for how much we should give.

Care to wager a guess as to why? Because it's good for budgets! It's good for sanity. If a church organization knows it can count on a certain number of dollars each week, it can do things like get everyone paid, build big pretty buildings and afford the nice paper. I don't even think it's malicious in most cases. Sure, there are wolves out there, but for the most part, I believe the reason many churches push this "faithful giving" mentality—the one that says tithing equals obedience, and God will return the favor in 90 days or your money back—genuinely just haven't approached it from the right vantage. They're not stupid. They're just sticking with what's plausibly biblical, causes very little friction and generally seems to work.

Imagine, for a moment, a church with no payroll. No one with any personal skin in the game, in terms of livelihood. What's the money for? Well, we can probably start with internal needs (and I'm talking about members in a legitimate bind). Then maybe local and community outreach … Aaand that's all, folks! Church budget done. Think about the connectivity behind something like that. People literally get to see their gifts put to work right before their eyes. And when it's time for the church to meet the needs of the local community, the opportunity is presented to everyone, and the level of response determines the aid provided.

Consider where the concept of church payroll comes from in the first place. The Levites were paid to help the priests facilitate worship in the Old Testament temple. Maybe that's how we've justified it? Some might say, "Well, churches need to compensate staff members and pastors for the work they do. It's hard to maintain that level of operation." Yeah, I guess. But we're talking about decentralizing those responsibilities and putting them back where Jesus intended them to be—with his ministers; his new temple (that's you and me). We can rack our brains for hours, trying to justify salaried leaders, but it will

always come back to someone having too much responsibility and needing to be compensated for doing everyone's job.

It's capitalism at its finest, man. The passively-motivated kind. Most churches aren't out to be cash cows, it's just the model we know in the West. Build it bigger. Make it stronger. Spread it wider. Why *wouldn't* we grow church organizations to utterly unmanageable ends? It's our nature! Our default setting is to take things into our own hands and pay out for the quick and dirty. Just because an organization might take twenty years to earn megachurch status doesn't mean it's healthy. Someone is still getting paid either to do too much work or not enough.

There's a popular stat that claims 20% of congregants pay for 80% of the operation (or something to that effect). That's not cool. And the way to solve it isn't by teaching people to be more obedient. In most cases, the solution is for churches to stop doing 80% too much! That's right. Maybe your church —like the one I pastored—is throwing a quinceañera for a ten-year-old. You've got programming suited for an organization of thousands but not enough maturity to glue it all together. Your spiritual giants are tapped out. So scale back. Downsize. Find where your little cell of the church body does its best work, and don't demand that it be anything more until it needs to be. My friend Josh Crute authored a children's book, called *Oliver*, about the second largest sequoia tree on earth. The lesson it taught me—you worry less about seeing through the trees when you realize you're part of a greater forest…

The problem is that church "generosity" generally finds motivation in strange places. And this is true for both pastor and parishioner. If all we were concerned with was helping each other and aiding our communities, we'd care a lot less about making the offertory count. We'd just let God move where he wants and use what he provides. But that's not all we think about. We've got our own mouths to feed and cars to fuel and mortgages to pay. So churches drive profitability and sustainability. That way, pastors and staff get paid for the work they do, and we end up forming the wrong kind of symbiotic relationship. Attenders give from pressure to be obedient (and reap that hundred-fold, 90-day return), while pastors maintain

a strong but tastefully implied undercurrent culture of tithing. And a workable exchange is brokered.

What kind of "generosity" is that teaching us though? Pay ten percent—pay it on time and in full—and enjoy the bonus blessings of zero guilt, less pastoral nagging and the added challenge of trying to discern where exactly you received your return on investment? I peddled the 90-day return policy in the church I pastored and actually had a few honest folks come forward to say they didn't feel like God had held up his end. It was then my duty to try and help them see the alternative ways in which God faithfully repaid their tithe dollars. Sometimes, it was a stretch. I'd even go as far to point out their good health over the last 3 months. But the truth is, God doesn't observe the weird manmade time constraints we impose on him. He's God. He provides. That's his story. There's no rulebook for how, why or when.

That's how the church could operate. Complete and utter dependence on God to provide for the needs of the body and the communities they support. We're either too afraid he won't come through, or we've gotten too accustomed to the church operating like a place of business. What if no one worked at your church? What if, instead, it was just a community of believers doing what they could to encourage and provide for each other, while also being a light and resource to those around them? So you have to get a real job. Big deal. I did it. You can too. That part should be the least concerning. The next challenge is about hearts conditions...

5. DITCH THE OFFERTORY

Stop passing the plate. Maybe that means you can't afford staff members. So what? It takes more effort to cook a Thanksgiving dinner than it does to be a functioning church body. And families do that for free. Appoint some cooks, table-setters and dish-washers and start feeding folks. Both figuratively and literally. Churches don't require full-time staff. They don't require mega-budgets. They require oversimplification. See the need and meet it.

While we're on the topic of necessity, it should be further established that God doesn't need your money. He needs your heart. And giving from the heart is always far easier and far more worthwhile when done from a place of raw response. I'm not talking about emotion. I'm talking about personal sacrifice and self-denial, where worship has nothing to do with reward.

"A time is coming and has now come when the true worshipers will worship the Father in the Spirit and in truth." —Jesus

BUTTERFLIES

It was a typical Sunday morning in the church of my adolescence. We were starting the twelfth or thirteenth song of our post-sermon worship set, when I felt the overwhelming call to remove my bass and leave the stage. It was the kind of church where you could do that sort of thing. Where the occasional need to come up for air was understood. Especially if you planned on surviving those protracted musical segments without wetting yourself in front of God and everybody. But I wasn't going to the bathroom. I was leaving. For good.

Something wasn't sitting right with me, even then. Something about the idea of playing and playing until we eventually crested whatever illusive spiritual plateau we were trying to reach. (I would later learn how to get people there inside four songs, but we'll address that in a moment.) At an early age, I learned that playing music in church was a great way to avoid just about any type of boring element, uncomfortable ritual or sudden spotlight. It was easy—hiding in plain sight. It also had the added benefit of being mentally and emotionally stimulating. That was the part I became addicted to, even if it was *my* job to get everyone *else* hooked.

I came up in a generation of church musicians who quickly latched onto the changes happening in worship world and weren't going to settle for anything else. Even if that meant leaving the motherland. It only took a few visits at churches in bigger cities to ruin me, opening my eyes to the concepts of professional production, intentional worship programming and excellent players who found real purpose in what they did each weekend. It was easy to see there was a glaring disjoint between what I was involved in and what else was out there.

It was this same splinter cell of young divergent musicians who would, just a few short years later, become the single biggest guerrilla union of guns-for-hire the modern church has ever seen or solicited. They had something everybody wanted, and they came in short supply. At a time when every church in America was dying to provide a rock 'n' roll worship set at the top of each service, money was quicker than personal development. Think about it—if your church is one of twenty in a city striving to have live music every weekend, and there are only ten worship guitarists in the area worth their salt, you're breaking out the checkbook.

I had friends who pocketed hundreds of dollars each weekend, answering bids from different churches to show up on time, be well-rehearsed and execute their parts masterfully. It was an absolute racket. And churches were happy to shell out more than their competitors in order to secure the best players for their programs. We talked about them like they were stocks

to be traded. "Did you hear Kevin scored Easter at Destination? It's like a thousand dollar Sunday." "Yeah, but they only pay in Target gift cards. You should try to get on at Seagrass Fellowship. They're set-up and tear-down, but they don't ask you to help unless you're a member." "Yeah, and I heard no one even talks to you as long as you know your parts."

You think it's crazy, but it might as well be a transcript. Thankfully some of the poison has been sucked out recently, due to members of that faction either accepting staff positions or giving up the scene entirely, but it still happens on a wide scale. From the outside looking in, it's easy to assume the issue is with these mercenary musicians, who seem to have made it exceedingly difficult for churches to provide just a baseline worship experience for their congregants without greedily demanding to be paid for their supposedly "unique" talents. It's a good theory. And it's completely wrong.

The issue—and I say this with informed certainty—is that there are churches who wholeheartedly believe it's their obligation to procure a top notch worship encounter for their people at any expense. Including that of actual people who are treated with such a hands-off, contractual approach, that they never truly feel at home in the places they serve. Why would they? In their eyes, and in the eyes of those watching, they're often nothing more than a single serving of disposable lubricant, used for a one-off intimate experience, before being paid and unceremoniously shown the door.

That's a brutal analogy. I get it. And if I could have drawn a different one, I would have. But nothing quite suits the situation the way sex does. Think about what's really happening here. A drummer is contracted to show up at an unfamiliar location, at a specific time, fully prepared to perform with expertise. When he arrives, he has a little bit of time to set up before the guest shows up to solicit the service he provides. For the guest, it's all about emotions—hitting that climax of spiritual butterflies within the span of three to five songs. Afterward, the drummer collects his payment and promptly leaves. There is no expectation that the church (or guests) provide anything further for the drummer. Just as there is no

expectation that the drummer stay and hear a message or try and create any lasting relationship with the guests.

You might say, "Well, it's different at my church…" or "I get paid to play, and I've never felt like that." Praise God. I'll accept a check for playing a special event (and I won't even feel dirty), but I've seen too many of my friends enlist where the money is, only to have their image of the church royally screwed forever. They're blown out. Likely to never return to the world of musical worship. I'm not saying it's impossible—kinda like how it's not impossible for a former porn star to cultivate a healthy relationship—but it might be hard to commit to a body they're used to pleasing with no strings attached (and do it for free). If you're a pay-to-play worship musician, hear me out— you are not your instrument; you are a son.

Hang in there. We're not even to the root of the issue yet. The problem with corporate worship in the twenty-first century isn't that people are paid to play us to a place of spiritual focus. The problem is that we believe the lie that says that's all worship is! In the West, worship is a forty-five minute event that happens once a week (or sometimes more, if you do Spotify in your car). It happens in a certain place, under certain circumstances that can only be curated by the church or those specifically anointed with great voices and the ability to speak poetically between songs. We wait expectantly, salivating all week long for the chance to just get back to that place where we encounter God's Spirit in the presence of his saints.

A lot of this book is addressed directly to church leadership, but this part is for you, dear member. Take careful inventory of the emotions you seem to be experiencing while partaking in your once-a-week spiritual pilgrimage back to neutral. Look at the lights, the haze, the stage design. Listen to the keyboard pads, those fancy boutique guitar pedals, the vocal reverb. Can you recall another time in your life when the same environment-setting techniques were deployed to give you a similar emotional experience? I can think of several: a Coldplay concert, an Avengers movie premiere, a Broadway show, a Netflix documentary about climate change, a high school dance, a night club, a music festival, Disney World. It's

ANNOINTING FIRE CONVICTION

OCEANS ANOTHER TEARS GOLD
          CHORUS   DUST

HOLY GHOST BUSTER

dangerously reminiscent of emotional manipulation.

Churches don't like to think of it that way. They like to think of it as clearing the way of distractions—giving people the best chance to have an encounter with God. I'm sorry, what?! Since when is my "God encounter" contingent on proper mood setting, geographical locations or time constraints? Since when is God something to be encountered only on occasion?

I get it for newcomers. Introduce them to a special, reserved time of reverent observation, introspection and admiration of their creator. But what is everyone else doing? Worship isn't about encountering a God you're not somehow already encountering. The life experience is a worship experience. Every second of every day. Yes, enjoy the music. Sing, shout, dance, but do it with the understanding that you are cheated if you believe that's all there is.

Music is easy. Mood is easy. Worship—true worship—is a workout. It's focus. It's self-denial. It's the culmination of all the little decisions and forfeitures you make during the week. It probably has less to do with Sunday or music than anything else. Every time you die to yourself, believing that God's plan is better than whatever short-term, temporal pleasure stands before you, you worship. Every time you acknowledge God's completed work *in* you and stop trying to atone for your own sins, you worship. Every time you acknowledge your true paternal origin, you worship. Every time you serve someone else, revel in the beauty of creation, or sit and listen for God's voice in stillness, you worship.

We are trapped in a self-serving, emotional loop of experiencing one encounter after another after another, and it has to stop. Helping people understand exactly why they no longer need the drug you provide—the one you got them hooked on—will be key. All it takes is your entire life…

6. DITCH THE MOOD

Emotional manipulation only goes so far. It's not a "win" just because someone cries or laughs during the service. It's only proof that people are awake. Congrats. The real mark of a church that worships is one that stays broken. There's no need to create a mood, because the focus isn't on fixing "me" or having an encounter. The focus is on Jesus, who constantly shatters our misconceptions about procedure and dependence and formula. Put away the checkbook. Put away the idea of perfect production, and worship in spirit and in truth.

JUGGERNAUT

I'll end this book the way I started it—with a blunt statement: the biggest thing missing from the church today is real discipleship. If that doesn't seem like a revolutionary proclamation, it's probably because the word—*discipleship*—doesn't mean that much to you. If it did, you'd be incredibly offended by such a claim. And rightly so. To say the church—*your church*—sucks at reproducing spiritual giants should come as a lethal swing. You should be up at arms at the mere insinuation of it. After all, if you're not showing, you're only telling. So, besides defensively flapping your lips, what are you going to do to prove me wrong?

Let's talk about those bright flares you've got burning right now. The ones who do whatever you ask and show up to everything. They're on the front row, hands up, voices loud. They're the ones you think of when you need someone to pray or speak publicly with the kind of Christianese that won't embarrass you or wreck your brand (they probably dress pretty cool, too, because they stay current on what the Australians are doing). Yeah, those. Are they deep or wide? Meaning, if you executed every experiment in this book—ditching the building, the platform, the paper trail, the weekend, the offertory and the mood—are they sticking around? Do they have the fortitude, right now, to continue to grow without you?

There are two kinds of discipleship concept. The first makes us think of small groups, Sunday school, Bible studies or coffee meetings with a mentor. Then there's the kind Jesus modeled, which was one of limited responsibility and expansive availability. Meaning, he knew the limits of what he was willing to take on before passing the torch, and yet every aspect of his person was easily accessible. It's the kind of drastic overexposure we don't quite grasp in the West. The kind that invites someone to penetrate our lives at every level. And quite frankly, we're not interested, even if we're the ones being mentored. It's awkward. Actually, it's beyond awkward. It's invasive, it's counterintuitive, and it feels a little like terrorism.

As a result, we tend to practice discipleship in a format we still find mildly annoying but a little easier to swallow. If we're doing it remotely right, we'll make a few touches per week, with someone, to either give or receive bite-sized servings of wisdom. We might text, call, or even keep each other accountable with weird spy software. That, alone, is exhausting. Not to mention, it can feel like a waste of time because of expectations placed on the parties involved. If someone shows up without reading their chapter—waste of time. If someone bails because life is hard or their alarm clock "randomly decided it didn't want work this morning!"—waste of time.

MY
MENTOR

ME

If we're doing it wrong, we'll start with a formulaic cocktail of devices just meant to get people in the door. You know—sh*t millennials like—Instagramable vistas, EDM, high-energy interactions, cake pops. Next we prime the emotions. Four melodramatic songs showcasing some semi-questionable doctrine (some real "Jesus is my boyfriend" bangers). Follow it up with a baby food TED talk, featuring some *fire* requotables, and wash it all down with your once-a-week shot to "get right." Then you leave. You just leave…

The problem with discipleship—modern, Western discipleship as we know it—is that we leave. Our faith is compartmental, because our discipleship is compartmental. Meaning that inside the four walls of a church, or within the context of our "spiritual" friendships, we see ourselves as new creations. We accept it. We believe it. While outside those parameters, we forget our spiritual identity and easily fold to the first set of extenuating circumstances that present the slightest bit of a challenge. Prayer Samurai on Sunday morning, loudmouth tool on Monday. It's not that we're two-faced, we just don't observe the fluidity.

Here's another way discipleship gets dismembered, bagged and zip-tied for its long journey to the sea floor... Mentors build barriers. Let's say you want to take it further than the weekend. Let's say you feel inspired to disciple someone with some added practicality. You might invite them to eat with you, drink with you, watch a game with you. You might even dedicate one morning a week to a focused study with that person or perhaps take a small group of people under your wing. But let's be honest, that's as close as they're gonna get. They won't see you working things out with your spouse. They won't see you stewarding your money. They won't see your integrity being tested in your day-to-day interactions.

Someone, somewhere, told you discipleship was safe. That it's done in a vacuum. Some church said, "That's alright, we'll take it from here..." and turned it into another metric. But the simple fact is that you can't *math* a church's effectiveness in discipleship when it's practiced at the level it was meant to be practiced. No church can take credit for that. It melds into real life. Slips between the countable cracks. There's a reason churches don't count the children of a family unit in their "Small Group Numbers" spreadsheet. They don't acknowledge that it's probably the *only* place actual discipleship is happening within their body. *"Children are our future!"* —Detached Pastor.

So what am I suggesting? That you should invite someone to live with you? That you should have the same people over for dinner on multiple nights of the week? That you should stay in constant communication with one person, taking an in-depth interest in the everyday events of their life? Well ... yeah, kind of. That's what the church is! And here's some good news—if you're a parent, grandparent, older sibling or obvious leader in a group of your peers, you already have the opportunity built-in.

Just be intentional. All it takes is realizing the weight of influence that your observable actions have with the people watching you. Share everything. Share it often. You'll have plenty of opportunities for privacy (a privilege you were never promised, by the way). If you're none of these things, your situation might look a little different…

Find the individual God has already made glaringly obvious in your life. Notice I say "the" individual, not "an" individual. It's not an Easter egg hunt. God doesn't make it hard to be the church with someone. He makes it annoyingly clear. Open your eyes. There's someone there already.

Don't be creepy about it, either. It's not a marriage proposal. It starts with being a genuine friend. As friendships strengthen, spiritual maturity rises to the surface. And that's when the awarenesses begin to take place. Both the awareness that your life is one to be modeled, and the awareness that your life is under someone's impressionable scrutiny.

It somehow seems easier now, doesn't it? The idea that discipleship is nothing more than a long-term friendship with an intentional emphasis on imparting spiritual maturity from one person to another. So why are we still producing such frail little Christians who break or bail when released into the real world? It's like one professor buys them a drink, or they read

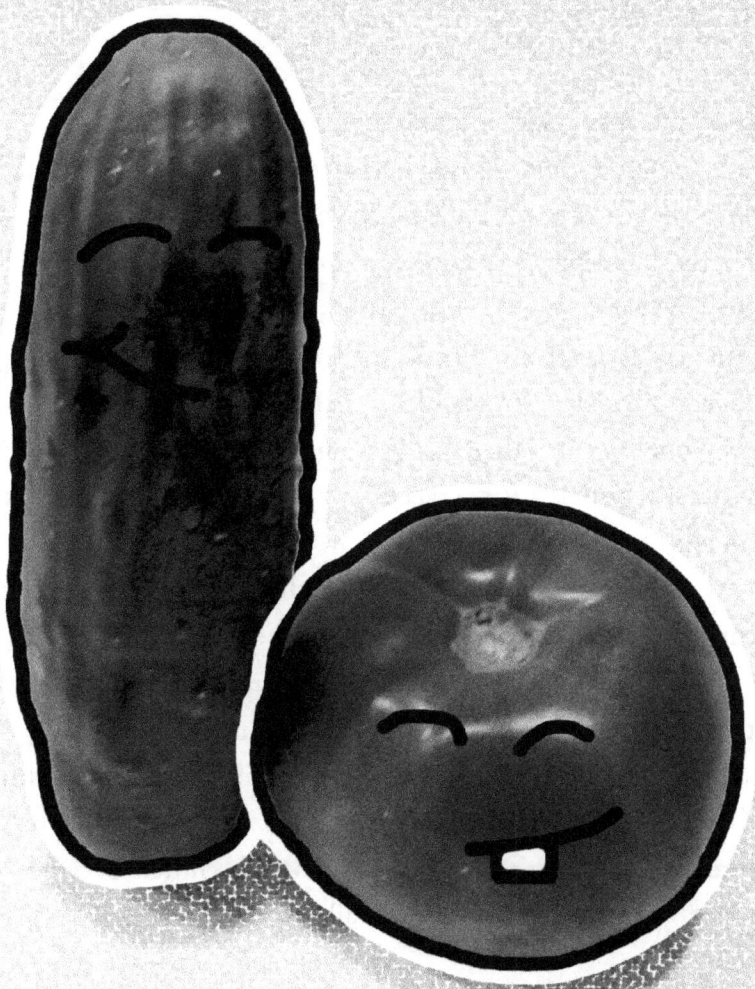

one Hitchens book, and they're just gone.

I'm convinced this occurs most frequently with people who weren't sold on the concept of sin. Instead they were sold on the concept of fighting surface-level, moral battles (which they eventually lose). And I think this happens most often in churches that are more concerned with being culturally relevant than spiritually strong. In other words, they either want everyone to like them (adopting stances that are about as biblically firm as a Ritz cracker), or they focus all their attention on battling the symptoms rather than the sickness.

Ask any former flare why they walked away. Talk to them long enough and you'll get to the truth. It's always some aspect of Christianity or God—some requirement of belief—that they just couldn't abide. And it's usually indicative of a symptom. They can't get behind the Bible's stance on this or that. It's the first sign of someone who never learned a broken heart for sin. If it's not that, it's that the church became God and failed them, and thus God failed them.

So here's your final dare. Forget everything you think you know about discipleship. When the finery is stripped away, when the systems are gone and the formulas are disproven, what you're left with are people. People with a common mandate: "Go and make disciples..." It's about as active as commissions get. You can't do it in a vacuum. You can't do it under a heat lamp. You do it person-to-person. Day-to-day.

MORE →

7. DITCH THE INCUBATOR

When your hands come off, and you give it all up, you can choose to see things one of two ways: either you lost your ability to control the temperature and grow the church yourself, or you just unleashed an overwhelming force—a juggernaut—capable of reaching deep and wide. Further than the church has gone in centuries. Should we keep track of each other? Sure. Discipleship is what holds it all together. Not bricks. Not systems. Not you.

Paradigm shifts don't happen overnight. *Movements* do. *Rebellions* do. *Fashion trends* do (sorry, there won't be any "Ditch the Building" buttons or ribbons or trucker hats). The point here isn't to be revolutionary. The point is to be the church as intended. That, alone, is revolutionary. If Jesus is part of you, your existence negates the need for a physical temple. You are the temple. That's why this is so important.

People are catching on. If leaders don't lead out, individuals will. And instead of saying, "It can't be done" you'll be asking, "Why have I chosen this hill to die on?" One day soon, when the sting wears off (and it will), when the sanctuaries are empty, we'll wonder why we ever trapped ourselves inside them in the first place. One day, when the church is rogue and giants roam the earth again.

CREDITS

RAM STATUE
*Artist: Unknown - A Photograph I took near
the Chattanooga Riverwalk Bridge*

ANTHONY BOURDAIN MURAL
*Artists: Nate Lyle and Brandon Barnhart
A photograph I took near downtown Pensacola*

CONCENTRIC CIRCLES
*A diagram concept borrowed from
Saddleback Church (which I heavily altered)*

BIKINI CONTEST PHOTO
*Photographer: Unknown - Spinnaker Beach Club
Panama City Beach, Circa 1990*

MAN AND HORSE STATUE
*"Man Controlling Trade" Artist: Michael Lance
A photograph I took near the FTC in Washington, D.C.*

GHASTLY MENTOR
*A photograph by Nathan Parens, featuring
a heavily-altered inclusion of Eleanor Roosevelt*

NICK MAY is an author and former church planter from Florida, where he lives with his wife (Kayla) and dog ("Brother"). Write him or view his other work at heynickmay.com.

www.ingramcontent.com/pod-product-compliance
Lightning Source LLC
LaVergne TN
LVHW061258060426
835508LV00015B/1409